THE NURSING HOME DILEMMA

BY THE AUTHOR

Don't Take My Grief Away: What to Do When You Lose a
Loved One
Comforting Those Who Grieve: A Guide for Helping Others

The Nursing Home Dilemma

How to Make One of Love's Toughest Decisions

Doug Manning

1817

Harper & Row, Publishers, San Francisco

Cambridge, Hagerstown, New York, Philadelphia
London, Mexico City, São Paulo, Singapore, Sydney

FIRST HARPER & ROW EDITION PUBLISHED IN 1985
This book is the expanded and adapted version of a booklet entitled WHEN LOVE GETS TOUGH: *The Nursing Home Decision.*

Library of Congress Cataloging-in-Publication Data

Manning, Doug.
  The nursing home dilemma.

  1. Nursing homes—Admission.   2. Decision making.
I. Title.
RA997.M355   1985   362.1'6   85-42783
ISBN 0-06-065425-2

85   86   87   88   HC   10   9   8   7   6   5   4   3   2   1

To Millie Belcher
and Sarah Young

Contents

Preface

There is no way to make the nursing home decision easy. Most of the time it is a decision we would like to avoid. At best it may be a choice between distasteful options. We make the decision out of necessity instead of choice.

The decision can be made with less guilt and fear if we can understand the reasons for the choice. We can live with the decision if we grasp the adjustment process loved ones experience when they begin a new life in a nursing home.

This book proved to be both the most difficult and the easiest one I have written. It was difficult because the nursing home decision is difficult. It was easy because the challenge and opportunity of making the decision easier to live with proved to be exciting.

This book carries the hope of enabling people to discover and consider the normal feelings experienced by those making this important decision. If it helps people feel normal and relieves guilt, then the book will have fulfilled the dream of the author.

Credit for this book must be given to Millie Belcher and Sarah Young, who gave birth to the concept; to Carolyn Baxter, who once again proved to be the typist who cares; to Bill Shields, the finest of editors; and to my wife, Barbara, who once again served as midwife while I tried to give birth.

I. MAKING THE DECISION

1. Love Is Doing What People Need—Not What They Want

I wish I had a nickel for everytime I have said, "My folks will never go to a nursing home." My exact words were, "I know there is nothing wrong with nursing homes, but neither my parents nor my wife's parents will ever go to one of them. They will have a home in my home for as long as they live." That was my boast. Last year my mother-in-law spent the last months of her life in a nursing home. My parents now live in a retirement center. The chances are very good that one of my parents will one day live in a nursing home. I am now eating crow.

I have gone through some rather drastic changes in my thinking. I am not alone in this change. Most of us never intended to place our parents in a nursing home. Most of us have made statements similar to mine, only to be forced to face the unreality of our boast. It is not an easy change to make. It is never made without guilt and fear.

My change came gradually. It began with an observation. Our neighbor could not face the thought of her mother going to a nursing home. Her mother lay in a coma and required constant care. These folks had to build a new house in order to accommodate the needs of her mother. Fortunately, they were financially able to construct such a home.

After the house was built and the family settled, it became evident that the wife could not handle the demands of such care on a full-time, twenty-four-hour basis. She had to have some relief. The answer was for her to get a job to get out of the house at least part of the time. The wife went to work, and a nurse was hired to take care of the mother during the day.

This provided some relief during the day, but the wife's schedule was still almost more than a human could bear. She worked at a full-time job outside the home and then returned to be the homemaker and the night nurse until time to go to work the next day.

I watched the effect of this plan over a period of four years. The wife did not have to face the guilt of placing her mother in a home, but the cost of avoiding this guilt was giving up her whole life. She thought she was doing all this for her mother. In reality she did it for herself. She desperately tried to avoid the guilt of a hard decision.

The husband was also affected. He had very little life of his own. The house became his whole world. There could be no vacations, no nights out, no weekends off. Every decision had to be made in light of how care could be provided for the mother. The mother's life had limited quality. Her presence in the home diminished the quality of life for everyone else.

Perhaps the most tragic figure in this drama was the wife's father. The neighbors lived next to us for several months before I knew the father even existed. His whole life consisted of sitting in a room next to his comatose wife and watching television. He had no one to talk with. He participated in no social activities. He just sat and withered away. We moved from the city before this story ended. I always thought the father would probably die before the mother. He seemed dead already as far as any quality of life was concerned.

There I was with my vow to never place a loved one in a nursing home while living next door to a tragic example of the disastrous results this vow could cause. My thoughts began changing.

The final change in my thinking came when we moved my mother-in-law into our house. She stayed only one week. One week convinced me that our decision was not in the best interest of my mother-in-law nor our family. My mother-in-law came to the same conclusion and suggested that something had to be done.

Nothing in our house fit the need. Our bathroom doors would not allow entrance to a wheelchair. The bath fixtures were not equipped for an elderly person.

We found ourselves tensely walking on eggshells. We could not be noisy. Our meals were not the right type for her.

It became evident we could not meet her needs— not even the evident physical needs. Nor could we provide for her emotional or social needs. Our world failed to match her world and her needs. We wanted to meet them. We loved her deeply. She was a dear lady.

It became evident to my wife and me that we had to make a decision based upon her mother's needs. The decision could not be based on making us feel good about ourselves. We had to face the fact that no matter how much we might care or how much we wanted to help, we just could not provide for the special needs of our loved one.

Love is doing what people need—not just what they want. Love is doing what people need—not what *we* want. In spite of what she wanted or what we wanted, we decided to place her in a nursing home. A nursing home could provide what we could not. Such things as round-the-clock nurses on duty, bath facilities designed for her, social contact with people with similar interests, and activities designed for people of her age and her condition would be provided for her.

We found a nursing home in our city. The home was equipped and seemed to have all the facilities she would need. Before we made the final decision, she had to be hospitalized. After a lengthy stay in the hospital she was moved to a nursing home.

It was still not easy. The nursing home seemed to be a strange setting for all of us. The roommate presented a problem. The adjustments we all had to make were still ahead of us. The only thing that helped us was the knowledge that we had no other option if her needs were to be met.

We clung to the idea that love is doing what people need. If we loved this lady, we had to make this tough decision and live with it.

On the surface it seems that love would mean we would care for our loved ones at home no matter what the cost. This might be true if the cost was ours alone. The fact is the cost is not ours alone. The people we take into our home must also pay a cost. It costs their privacy. It costs them social contact. It costs them the meeting of their physical needs. They may never recognize these costs. They may never agree with the decision. They may never see the wisdom of the decision. When they do not understand or agree, we still must make the decision based on what is best for them as we see it.

It is not an easy decision under the best of circumstances. It is a terribly hard decision when the loved one does not agree. The only comfort I found and the only comfort I could give was for us to concentrate on the needs and provide for them.

2. When Love Gets Tough

We had no choice when my mother-in-law entered the nursing home. After nine weeks in the hospital, the only alternatives were continued hospitalization or the nursing home.

Some cases allow more options and therefore, more choices. Perhaps a loved one is still mobile, but can no longer live alone. Perhaps a death brings about the need for a change in living arrangements. Perhaps aging creates the need for a look at the future living arrangements. Perhaps the distance between the loved one and the children creates a problem, and it is evident this distance needs to be eliminated. These situations create tough decisions.

When I was faced with these options I chose to take my mother-in-law into my home. There are times when this choice works well, and I was ready to try. I was not ready to face the nursing home decision and certainly was not ready to confront my mother-in-law with this choice. By suggesting the need herself, she saved me from the choice. Looking back, I must say that in our case the choice was correct. Any other choice would have made all of us miserable.

My mother-in-law would have been miserable because her whole routine of living would have changed. She would have had very limited freedom to do as she pleased. She would have had to eat when we ate and to eat what we ate. She would have had to sit through her evening with us or spend them alone in her room. She would not have felt free to have friends over.

She might have felt the need to make friends her own age, but there would have been limited social contact to help her make friends. We would have been there and would have been expected to fill the needs only friends can fulfill. In spite of any effort we might have put in, she would have been a guest visiting in our home. To live with us she might have had to make as many adjustments in her style of living as she would have if she had gone to a nursing home. The adjustments to living with us might well have been harder than the adjustments to a nursing home.

My wife would also have had some tough changes to make. How do you stop being a child to your parent and suddenly become the parent to your parent? This change must happen if there is to be peace in the house. There cannot be two mothers in the same house.

Parenting of a family must come from only one source. This source—whether a husband and wife or a single parent—provides the disciplining of children and the setting of life-styles. It has often been said, "A house is not big enough for two families." When a parent is added to the household, there is often a conflict created in the children. Suddenly, there are two sources trying to give input in vital areas. Handling this conflict requires tremendous compromises and changes. I doubt that these changes could have been made in our case.

Moving her into our house would have had an impact on our marriage. My wife and I have worked hard on our marriage over the years. Any marriage that lasts requires hard work. We have reached the age when we can do things together. We are also at the age we can drift apart. Many marriages become stale and even die during these years. We need time to be together, to travel, to talk, to plan, and to grow. If we fail now, we can look forward to some lonely years ahead. I can think of nothing more devastating to our relationship than another person always being present. This would be true no matter who the other person is. Even a child moving back home could be a problem.

Looking back, I fear that without her help, I would not have been tough enough to consider these complex issues. I probably would have moved her into our house and waited for the day when she became ill enough to justify moving her to a nursing home. I might have felt better about that postponed decision. I would not have had to face the guilt of the decision. I would not have done the right thing nor the loving thing.

If love is doing what people need instead of what they want, then sometimes love must be tough. Sometimes love must be short-term mean in order to be long-term kind. In such cases I should do what is best, no matter how much guilt I have to face as a result of doing it.

If I could have been tough enough to take the stand to move her to a nursing home even without her help, there would have been some positive benefits we all could have enjoyed. My mother-in-law would have benefited in several ways.

1. She would have been placed in a nursing home while she was able to adjust to a new home. She would have had adjustments to face no matter where she moved; to move her to our home and put her through the adjustments

there and then move her to a nursing home after she could not make further adjustments would have been double jeopardy. Too often people are put into nursing homes too late, and they never adjust. Much can be said for moving a family member to a nursing home while the relative still has the faculties and will to adjust.

2. She would have been mobile enough to make friends. One of the benefits my parents derived from moving to a retirement center was that they made friends. This has become a more important issue in our mobile society. Most elderly people do not have their children living in the city where they live. Most of the time they must move to a new city when the time comes to be near their children. This means they must leave their home and friends behind. If this move can be made early enough, they can find new friends. My parents have formed new friendships in the center where they live as well as in the city and in their church. If they had not moved early, the day would have come when they would have been moved here with no friends and no mobility to make friends.

3. She would have been forced to make friends. If she had lived in our home, the tendency might have been for us to take the place of friends. If we were not there, she would make friends for herself.

We also would have benefited from the early decision to move her to a nursing home. We would have had the freedom we needed without the worry of our loved one living alone in a city several hours away. We would have had the assurance that her needs were being met. She would have remained a mother instead of a burden.

This is not to say the decision would have been easy. My parents have had a rough time adjusting. No one should have to move at eighty years of age. They had lived in the same small town for fifty years. They were well known and deeply loved by the people in the town. They had position there. It was their turf. Now they must begin all over again. This has not been easy for them or me. I cling to the idea that if the adjustment can be made, it will be the best decision in the long run. The alternative was to leave them where they were until we were forced to move them. If we had waited that long, they would have had to leave their friends with no way to ever replace them.

If there had been options available when the decision was made about my mother-in-law, I do not know what I would have done. I know the loving decision would have been to find a place where her needs could have been met. Those needs could not have been met in our home.

I might have wished I could have kept my boast about never placing her in a nursing home, but the fact was I could not keep my boast. I could not build a home as my neighbor did. I could not afford nurses. I could not change our family's life-style. In the case of our family, I could not, in good conscience, put much of the responsibility of care on my wife.

Like it or not, the right thing would have been for us to find a comfortable, loving place and move her there. We should have found a nursing home that could meet her social, physical, emotional, and spiritual needs. This would have been the loving decision. Tough, yes. But loving, nonetheless.

3. Tough Love and Culture

Cultural attitudes and reality seldom move on the same timetable. Long after changes in society happen or are forced upon us, we still struggle with cultural patterns from the past. We are torn between the reality of the present and the leftover expectations of the past. The result is that we are forced to change our thinking and our actions, but we pay a price for each change. We end up with a great deal of inner conflict. We can tell ourselves the present situation demands a new way of thinking, but in the back of our minds we never seem to be convinced.

It is difficult to get over our upbringing. Things drilled into us as youngsters have a way of hanging on in our subconscious minds. They hang there long after we know reality's truth.

When I was young, they told us to never drink milk while eating fish. They said the combination would make us ill, or maybe even kill us. I now know there is nothing wrong with drinking milk and eating fish at the same time. I can understand where this idea got started. In the days before adequate refrigeration, people must have eaten spoiled fish or drunk bad milk. When they became ill, the only plausible explanation seemed to be that the milk-fish combination was deadly. They did not know about bacteria, germs, and viruses. They knew drinking milk and eating fish at the same time made them sick.

The idea is gone now. I have not heard it in years. But even with all of this knowledge and the passage of time, I still have a hard time drinking milk when I am eating fish. Cultural attitudes and reality rarely move on the same timetable.

There is no area where attitudes have lagged behind more than in the case of nursing homes. Our culture seems to tell us we are responsible no matter what the situation. It says we must care for our loved ones no matter what the cost. It further says the only loving care takes place in our own homes. If we fail to take family members into our homes, we have "put them away in a nursing home" and therefore do not love them. Something in the back of our minds says, "For shame." These attitudes will die slowly. Long after we know better, we will be struggling with the hangover guilt in the same way I struggle with milk and fish.

We can at least acknowledge that these attitudes come from a different era. They are not based on current reality. Placing a loved one in a competent nursing home is nothing like hauling that person off to the county poor farm of years ago. There is no comparison, but the cultural attitudes we face are about the same.

We need to realize that times have changed, and our attitudes must change. To this old attitude I want to shout, "Hey, we are talking about a different day with different problems and different situations." Some of the differences follow.

DIFFERENT GEOGRAPHY.

We are now a scattered society. In the past if a family had several children, some of them would remain in the general area of the hometown. As the parents aged, these children could share the care and not place a major burden on any one family.

In this day there are rarely any children near the family's hometown. In some cases, there may be one who stayed home while the others scattered to the four winds. The one who stays home automatically assumes the responsibility of caring for the parents. This assuming of responsibility is often not appreciated by the other children. The result can be hard feelings and chaos.

Since there is a scattered family, the parents will probably have to move. If they are moving, they might as well adjust to a nursing home where they can make friends as we discussed in the last chapter.

If there are children in the town, it does not mean the parents should not go to a nursing home. The logic of their doing so remains the same no matter what the geography may be.

DIFFERENT NUMBERS.

A simple look at the life expectancy changes over the years will show the need for a new attitude. People live longer now than ever before in history. More people live longer now than ever before in history.

I am fifty years of age. There was a time not so long ago when I would have been considered old. If I had a parent living at my age, I would have been considered lucky. If I had both parents living at my age, I would have been considered rare. If I had both parents and both in-laws living, I could have made Ripley's "Believe It or Not." The sheer numbers of people living into their seventies or eighties now forces us to rethink our old attitudes. In earlier days if someone moved a loved one into a home the arrangement was expected to be short-lived because the life span was short. There is a big difference between five years of care and twenty years of responsibility. If I take a loved one into my home now, I am making a much longer commitment of my life.

In earlier days I would have been fortunate to have had to face the long-term care of a single loved one. The chances of having to face this with more than one person would have been rare. It is not rare now to face caring for four loved ones at the same time. My father-in-law died of cancer, or I could have faced this four-some problem last year. Numbers alone have made me rethink my boast about none of my loved ones going to a nursing home.

DIFFERENT FACILITIES.

There were such places as county poor farms. These were squalid charity facilities where folks went or were sent to wait for death. I do not know how horrible they actually were. These places were dreaded more than prison. The worst thing that could happen to anyone was to have their children haul them off to the county poor farm. These places and this fear created our attitudes about nursing homes. No matter how nice the facility, we still have the attitudinal hangover of taking our parents to the county poor farm.

Tonight I am going to speak at the nursing home in my city. I speak there once a month. I would not miss this event. I love the people there, and they love me. They are a great group. They are happy, busy, involved with each other, and very much alive. I have toured the facility many times. It is a clean, well-organized, well-staffed, and happy home for some fine people. It tries to meet the physical, social, emotional, and spiritual needs of these people. Most of the folks there are happy. There are, of course, those who are not happy. There are those who have not made the adjustment. There are those who have soured on life. These folks are to be expected, and they are exceptions.

As I walk through this home, I always wonder how we ever got such a negative attitude about places such as this. Why do we feel as if we have hauled our folks to the county poor farm when we place them in a facility with so much to offer to those who can enjoy it and so much to give to those who need care?

The attitudes will die slowly, but they will die. I told a young person about the milk and fish story, and he could not believe we ever gave any credence to such a tale.

HARD QUESTIONS

Maybe our archaic attitudes about nursing homes will also change. Until the change comes we must live with our decisions. Facing the decision will demand that we ask some hard questions and try to find some answers. Some of those questions follow:

WHAT IS MY RESPONSIBILITY?

What do I owe my parents? I owe them my love, understanding, and care. Do I owe them my life? Should I give up the living of my life to pay off some debt I owe?

If my parents gave up their lives for me, they were

wrong. If they lived their lives through me, they missed living.

When each of my four daughters graduated from high school, they had to listen to a speech from me. I told them I had invested a lot in their lives, but I had received a great deal from their lives. I told them we were even. I did not owe them, and they did not owe me. I intended to educate them because I believed in them, but I did not want them to live their lives trying to please me. They were free.

I gave them their freedom, but at the same time I claimed freedom for myself. We can love each other as equals and not as parent and child. I can enjoy their growth, their challenges, their living out their potential without having to feel responsible. I am free.

I want them to have lives of their own. I hope I never feel they owe me. I hope I never feel they are obligated to take care of me. I hope I never lose sight of all they have already given me. We are even. I do not owe my folks either. We, too, are even. I will love, care , understand, and be there, but it will not be out of debt or obligation or some sense of my life needing to be sacrificial because of their sacrifice.

WHAT WOULD I WANT DONE TO ME?

Jesus Christ said, "Do unto others as you would have them do unto you." We call this the golden rule. It is also one of the most practical statements ever spoken.

There are times when we have no clear-cut choice between good and evil. There are times when the only choice is the lesser of two evils. There are times when the world is not black or white. There are times when the whole thing is gray. When we face this kind of decision, the one practical aid is "How would I want to be treated?" This golden gem provides excellent guidance.

The nursing home decision is a lesser-of-two-evils type of choice. It would be better if parents could remain healthy and self-sustaining until they died. If that is not possible, then any alternative is not very desirable. The golden rule test asks the questions that clarify the issue:

Would I want my children missing their lives taking care of me?
Would I be comfortable in some one else's home?
Would I rather die than be a burden?

When I give the issue the golden rule test, I can readily see how I must decide. The next step is learning how to handle the guilt caused by cultural attitude.

II. IMPLEMENTING THE DECISION

4. Preparation

When the nursing home decision becomes inevitable, the work has just begun. As in most major decisions, too much deciding with too little preparation can lead to bad decisions and bad results. Too often the decision is made without adequate research into the actual need or the details such a decision inevitably creates.

If adequate research into the need of placement is not done, then an important area of support will be missing when the going gets tough and the doubts arise. We need to know that the nursing home was the best decision or the only decision possible.

If adequate planning is not done, there can be serious misunderstandings among family members. They only way to avoid misunderstanding is to have an understanding. Too often people assume there is a clear understanding when in reality an understanding does not exist. Too often people think because they are part of a family there will be no problems. Even close families can be torn apart by the guilt, fears, and the feeling of not having a voice in the decision. If adequate planning into the financial considerations is not done, there can be serious family problems, inadequate financing available, or tax problems caused by how the money is handled.

The planning needs to include research into the actual need, as complete an understanding with the family as possible, a full revelation to the person to be admitted into the home, and a realistic look into the finances available and the best way to administer these funds. It might prove helpful to look at each of these steps in more detail.

PROVING THE NEED

In a large number of cases the nursing home decision is brought up by the physician after a stay in the hospital. When the patient is well enough to leave the hospital, the doctor will usually inquire about the facilities available to the patient after the hospital stay. This leads to a discussion about the possibility of a nursing home.

During the hospital stay the family will probably have already mentioned the idea at least in a casual manner. When the doctor mentions the need, it confirms the suspicions and fears. Too often the family hears this as a final decision based on the doctor's orders. Family members proceed without further inquiry and place the patient in the home. The doubts come later.

When the patient is not adjusting well or the guilt begins to hit, then families tend to wonder if the doctor was correct or if they acted with too much haste. They wonder if there could have been a better decision. This needs to be worked through before the decision is made. When the doubts come, they need to be able to tell themselves that they looked at all the alternatives and that this was the best decision possible.

The doctor should give a full and understandable prognosis. Far too often doctors are not the best communicators. They tend to talk in hurried, guarded language while their body language screams that they are far too busy to have time for conversation.

Most people are intimidated by doctors. They promptly forget all the questions they wanted to ask. They get nervous and want the conversation to end. It usually ends without their knowing very much. After the doctor leaves the room, they think of all the questions they intended to ask and all the ones they needed to ask.

The importance of this decision demands that it be made with as much knowledge as possible. Write down the major questions. There is no way to list all these questions since each case will be different. Some general ideas as to the type of questions to ask follow:

1. You have suggested a nursing home. Does this suggestion mean my loved one is not going to improve enough in the long haul to be self-sufficient and be able to care for himself?

   However this is stated, what is being asked for is a long-term prognosis of what can be expected. The doctor may hedge at this. Do not be intimidated. Ask again until you are satisfied that you have received the best answer.

2. How much care does the patient need now? When do you think there will be need for more care?

   This sounds like the first question, but the aim is different. What must be determined is the kind of home to look for. If the patient needs special care, then a home with this type of care must be found. If there is a good chance that this care will be needed in the future, the family will then have to consider whether to start with a home that gives this care or plan on a move later, as the need develops.

3. When does the move need to be made?

With the new Medicare reimbursement system, the hospital can only receive payment for a certain period of time. Often this determines when the move must be made. The family needs to know the time limitations and the reasons for them. Later, when doubts come up, it is too easy to think back and decide there was too much haste and therefore, maybe the haste led to the wrong choice.

In addition to talking to the doctor, it might help to talk with the nurses, the aides, and the other hospital employees who have dealt with the patient. These people see the patient more often than the doctors and see them in a more normal setting. Often a patient will put on a front for the family and the doctor. These people can give valuable guidance about the need for a nursing home.

Many hospitals have social workers available to give counsel in this area. These professionals can be a great help in facing the reality and making the decision.

The decision made after a stay in the hospital and suggested by a doctor is tough, but the decision made without this encouragement and help is even harder to make.

Let's say a mother has been living alone and has gradually become less able to function. She wants to maintain her independence at all cost. She will usually hide her need from the family. The family knows all is not well, but the hard part is deciding how bad it is and how bad it must be before anything is done. Should we just let it ride until she falls and breaks a hip or becomes ill, or should we intervene before a disaster forces the issue?

We need to monitor the situation as it progresses to see the pattern of deterioration and the depth of the problem. A frank talk with her physician is in order. We need all the medical facts possible to know when the decision needs to be made.

A talk with her friends can prove valuable. They will know the facts far better than anyone else. They will know how forgetful she has become, how well she is eating and sleeping, and will often know about dizzy spells and other ailments she is hiding from her family and doctor.

Talk to her clergyman. He may not be intimately connected with her and therefore, not be in a position to give much help, but there are many cases when he will know and will have some thoughts about her condition and need.

Talk to the groceryman, the postman, the person who delivers papers, the one who cares for the lawn, the neighbor, or anyone else who has a chance to observe her regularly. This seems like spying, but it is not. It is building as complete a prognosis as possible. We need this prognosis when we make the decision and when we later wonder if we have made the right decision.

INCLUDING THE FAMILY

If ever there needed to be full agreement in a family, it is now. Too often the decision is left to one family member and the rest are left to second-guess.

If at all possible, there needs to be a family conference with every member possible physically present. It is totally unfair for the family to shove this decision off on one or two members because they happen to live nearby and therefore, know the situation. There are too many decisions involved, everyone of which provides too many opportunities for second-guessing.

The decision to place a loved one in a nursing home raises other questions that a family must agree on. These include financial and legal matters and such personal decisions as disposal of house, furniture, property, and private belongings. It is best if the whole family can be involved in reaching an agreement. If a physical meeting is not possible, then an exchange of phone calls and letters must suffice.

A good place to start when the family is together is a discussion of the condition of the loved one and the predicted health status to be expected in the future. This is the time for the whole family to face reality. Every member should be asked, if not required, to reveal true feelings. Too often the ones who say the least turn out to be the most critical. The spectator is always a potential critic.

Bill Russell, the famous basketball player, coach, and television broadcaster, says, "Always try to get the ball to the guy who is just standing around." Get the whole team involved. This is the goal of the family conference.

Whoever takes the lead should ask and ask again until the true feelings are expressed. There should not be arguments. No one likes arguments. All that can be accomplished by an argument is reluctant acquiescence. If folks are allowed to talk out their feelings, it is amazing how often they will talk their way into agreement. If they are attacked, they will build their defenses and sit there. Let them talk.

I received a letter from a woman who could not get her family to discuss the needs of their mother. One person took it upon herself to set up a schedule for each of the seven children to have the mother in his or her home for two-week periods. Could there be anything harder on this eighty-year-old mother than moving every two weeks from now on? The problem the woman wrote to tell me about was that she worked full time and could not take her turn. The rest of the family was incensed at her failure. I wonder how much better this family could have dealt with the needs of the mother if they could have gotten together and dealt with their feelings with openness and honesty.

Sometimes the decision is faced by an only child. This may be an even tougher experience than facing a large and even hostile family. The only child must make the decision alone and be responsible for the consequences. The only child does not have the support of others when the loved one must be told and the confrontations come. The only child does not have the confrontation sessions with family to clear the air and solidify thoughts and feelings.

It becomes almost necessary for the only child to form a surrogate family to help with the decisions. It will help to talk with a mate or friends, children or clergy, or ask the nursing home administrator for names of other only children who have faced this situation. This decision is far too tough to be made alone.

Perhaps one of the toughest decisions of all is the one made by a mate who must place a husband or wife in a nursing home. Nursing home personnel report that a husband placing a wife is probably the hardest of all. The husband seems to have an inborn urge to be the caretaker for the wife. It is a difficult thing to go against this natural urge and not feel like a failure or a traitor.

The nursing home decision needs either the family

or a surrogate family involved. Someone needs to be available to help talk through the decision and the feelings involved. Talking through the decision can do a great deal toward handling the guilt and feelings which can arise.

CONFRONTING THE PATIENT

Often the last person consulted about the nursing home decision is the person to be admitted. Few things can be harder than confronting a mother or father with the need for such a move. The natural tendency is to dread the ordeal and put off the confrontation as long as possible. In an effort to either protect them or us we tend to tell only part of the story. The usual result is the person is told the move is not permanent. This is not done to hurt the person. It is done with the idea that learning about the permanency a little at a time will make it easier. Our efforts at protection can end up causing more pain instead of less.

The person must be told the whole story and be allowed to respond. Those to be admitted will have feelings about the matter, and these feelings must be talked through if they are to be dealt with and be accepted. This is not the time for arguing, nor is it the time for our reaction to any guilt trips a relative may choose to use in an effort to avoid the decision.

The ideal situation is to confront the person with honesty and a clear explanation of the reasons for the decision. This needs to be followed by a full response from the patient. If the patient responds with guilt such as, "How could you do this to me?" or fear such as, "I had rather be dead than have to go to a nursing home," we need to recognize these as avoidance moves to keep from facing the issue. If we pick up on these avoidance tools, we end up arguing about these side issues instead of the real problem. If we do not pick up on the avoidance plays, the person ultimately must deal with the reality.

This process will not happen quickly. It must be done over a period of time. I met a woman recently who had tried for years to get up the courage to confront her mother. Everytime she would try, her mother would always manage to divert the daughter with guilt or fear. We talked about the method of staying with the issue instead of chasing the diversions. She determined to give it a try. It was not easy. The mother had controlled the daughter with guilt and fear all her life. The daughter finally began to confront her mother and was able to stay on the subject. When the guilt and fear did not work, the mother redoubled her efforts. The mother called in her sister to add to the guilt and fear. The daughter stayed firm, and gradually the mother began to deal with the issue. The daughter called me the other day and told me her mother had entered a nursing home, and though it seemed an impossible dream, the mother loved her new home.

This was made possible by taking the correct approach to the necessary confrontation. Avoiding this kind of confrontation can mean patients enter a new world with no preparation for the change in their lives and no way to work through their feelings.

This confrontation needs to happen no matter what condition the residents-to-be happen to be in. They may not be able to fully comprehend, but they should be told nevertheless. It may be that the explanation must be given again and again. It may be that their grasping of the issue will be partial and the matter will never be fully understood. Whatever they can grasp will create feelings, and they need to deal with whatever feelings they have.

Someone should even sit down and explain what will happen to a patient in a coma. We do not know how much patients in this condition can hear and understand. Even if they do not hear or comprehend, the experience will help work out the feelings of the one doing the talking.

It is tragic, but true, that a large number of people end up in nursing homes with false hopes about the length of their stay or even with no idea where they are or why they are in the place. Families may not be able to get complete agreement or understanding, but the effort must be made. This gives the only chance for feelings to be worked through and an understanding established.

DEALING WITH THE MONEY

The hard reality of the situation is that decisions must be based on what we can afford. This may seem to be a cold reality when dealing with the emotion of what to do with a loved one.

We must know the whole story of cost. Visit some nursing homes and find out what the total cost of care will be. The cost will vary with the type of care required. When figuring the cost, include the added costs that are often missed. These are not hidden costs in the sense that anyone is trying to put anything over on us. These costs are for the extras not included in the normal care. They include medicine, extra laundry, and extra nursing care required by the condition of the resident.

A full understanding is needed of the help possible through Medicare and Medicaid. These programs change regularly and have limits we need to understand. The administrators of nursing homes are well-informed on this subject. They can be helpful in explaining what to expect from this program.

Families need to know the full story of the patient's assets. It may seem inappropriate to discuss the subject at the time, but there is no other way to determine the financial needs and how they are to be met. Planning for the future must be done. Family members should know what assets can be sold. They also should know what income will be needed now and what might be needed in the future.

The planning might need to include what the family will have to contribute. This needs to be worked out before the fact. The family conference is the time for these decisions to be worked out and a complete understanding to be reached.

LEGAL ISSUES

When we placed my mother-in-law in a nursing home we took the line of least resistance. My wife opened a joint account with her mother. When her mother faced surgery, we transferred all of the mother's assets into my wife's name. This was done on the spur of the moment in the hospital with a notary public from the hospital business office.

We were fortunate. My wife's sister and brother were trusting and understanding. Had this not been the case, we could have faced tremendous family problems. The brother or sister could have decided my wife was not spending the money properly or that they were being ripped off. We did not even consider these possibilities and somehow avoided the problems. Others are not so lucky. Many families find themselves struggling over trying to handle the financial issues with no real thought to the safeguards necessary to avoid conflict.

Even though we escaped with no family problems, we did not avoid the problems with taxes. We are still trying to untangle all of the questions of ownership with the Internal Revenue Service.

The legal questions need to be faced no matter how wealthy or poor the patient may be. If all the patient has is Social Security, it is still a good idea to make proper provisions for handling the spending process.

Nursing home residents may currently be capable of handling the spending process for themselves. In a few years, or even sooner, the conditions may change. Planning needs to be done on how spending should be handled. It is a good idea to consult a competent attorney for advice and counsel. An attorney who deals with this type of problem can be found by calling the local bar association. It is a good idea to ask the fee for a consultation when the call for an appointment is placed.

The lawyer may suggest a trust agreement or some other simple mechanism for handling the estate. These do not need to be complicated or costly. They can avoid problems with family and the IRS.

At the same visit, ask about a will. This is a tough question to face at this time, and families dread talking about it. Dreaded or not, a will is almost an absolute necessity for avoiding problems in the future.

This chapter has been dedicated to distasteful details. The idea of confronting the family and the patient along with the idea of money and lawyers are all things families would rather avoid. If we avoid them now, they can hurt us in the future. The only way to avoid misunderstanding is to have an understanding.

5. The Choice

With all the decisions we were facing with my mother-in-law, I am glad we did not have to face a choice between nursing homes. There is only one home in our city, and it is a very fine facility. Normally this home is full and has a waiting list. When we had a need, there happened to be a bed available.

Most of the time a family will not be so fortunate. When there is a choice, we often find ourselves at a loss as to what factors to consider in the choice. Does location matter? Does it matter more than the type of accommodations or less? How important are such things as programs, hair salons, exercise, and entertainment? What about the food? Most families find themselves called upon to make a crucial decision with no clear idea about what things should enter into the choice.

Looking back on our experience, I often try to think through some "what ifs." What if the home in our town had been full? What if this home had been far less adequate than it is? What if the home here had been totally unacceptable? I have asked myself where we would have chosen for my mother-in-law to live and what would have been the determining factors.

A large Texas city is fifty miles from our community. This city has one of the finest nursing homes imaginable. It boasts of a new building decorated with the very best of taste and designed with the latest technology to do the best job possible in elderly care. This home has almost unlimited resources, great programs, a well-trained staff, and pleasant administrators. I am not sure there is a better facility anywhere.

This home would be toward the bottom of my list of possibilities. That may seem strange since it seems to offer so much. The problem is that while the home can offer almost everything a loved one could need, it cannot offer the most important factor to be considered in the decision. The distance between the cities would diminish the chance to see loved ones.

Fifty miles may not seem far, but it is far enough to limit the number of times we could be there. Try as we might, there would be too many things that could happen, too many last minute phone calls, too many meetings to attend, and often too much physical drain from the day. Our visits and our involvement would be limited by the distance. If the choice must be made between an acceptable home close enough for personal involvement and an exceptional home far enough away to limit personal involvement, I think the decision has to be cast in favor of personal involvement. In our case we found the most important part of the decision was us.

This came as a surprise to us. One of the major problems we have with nursing homes is our unfulfilled expectations. We tend to see these facilities as full-time hospitals designed for the elderly where everything needed is furnished and our role can be that of the occasional visitor. People who view a nursing home with this unrealistic expectation usually find themselves disillusioned and often bitter.

A nursing home is a home, not a hospital. Such homes are not in existence to remove responsibility from the family nor to replace the role of family in the life of the patient. Too often a nursing home is seen as a place hired to do all things for a patient while the family's role becomes one of seeing to it that the job is done correctly. This puts us in the role of a critic. There are times when we must criticize. It is amazing how much more we criticize when we are spectators instead of participants. It is also amazing how much more effective criticism can be when it comes from a participant.

Even in the best of homes it is still largely our responsibility. We will determine how the adjustment is made. The adjustment process is not related just to the new surroundings. It is related to our new roles, our continuing care, our support, and our presence.

Families are the link between the resident and the outside world. This world is still dear to the resident, and if contact is not maintained, they will feel cut off. The home can take care of physical needs far better than we can, but we alone can offer the continuing relationship with family and the continuing support needed for the resident to maintain a sense of security and purpose.

This may be the most important point in this book. If we can get a proper perspective on the role the nursing home can play and the role we must maintain, we can avoid unfulfilled expectations. These expectation levels tend to lead to disillusionment and despair.

If I had a choice between homes, I would choose with my own involvement as the number one criterion. An adequate home which allowed me to fulfill my role would serve the purpose better than a super home with my role diminished.

OTHER CONSIDERATIONS

I am sure a long checklist could be provided for a family to use as a scoresheet in judging a home. I am afraid the end result would be confusing and far from effective.

A visit to three homes is enough to make one a competent judge. There is a certain feel about a happy nursing home. This feel is hard to define and impossible to capture on a checklist. I have visited hundreds of homes in the last few years. The happy ones are not always the ones with the finest facilities or the best decorations or even the most programs. The happy ones have a feeling of happiness and peace that becomes apparent from the front door of the home. If we are properly prepared for the visit, we can pick up on the feel of the place for ourselves.

PREPARING FOR THE VISIT

Most of us have not spent much time in nursing homes. Most of the visits we have experienced have been short forays to see someone or perhaps to participate in a program sponsored by a church or club.

The first visit can be a shock. My first few visits were almost repulsive. I was unprepared for the experience of walking into the sitting area and being confronted with what seemed to be a sea of wheelchairs and sick people. My first thought was that these people should be hidden somewhere so I would not be confronted by the scene. I was uncomfortable, to say the least. I did not know what to say or do. I looked straight ahead, avoiding any eye contact and saying nothing. One lady reached for me and I drew back almost in horror. I left as quickly as possible. I felt foolish, repulsed, and guilty, all at the same time.

During my next visit to a nursing home I drew up my courage and prepared myself for the confrontation. This time I stopped to talk and reached out to touch. My fears and sense of aversion melted. What appeared at first to be wasted lives waiting for death became significant folks living in spite of their conditions and to the best of their abilities. They might have been ill and limited, but they were not going to waste away in some room. They were going to be as free as possible for as long as possible. Suddenly I caught the spark of the place and was no longer repulsed.

It may be necessary for us to go several times before we can speak and touch. The speaking and touching will not only brighten the day of the residents, it will help us face our fears.

INSPECTION

Once we have prepared ourselves for an inspection visit we can go with the objectivity we need to see and feel the place. Without making an actual check list there are some general things to notice. These general things fall into two categories, physical and attitudinal.

CLEANLINESS.

Is the place clean? I think you will find that most homes will be clean. State laws are very strict in this area. It is a reassuring factor for us to know the place is clean. Notice more than the floors. Is the place well dusted? Does it have a general appearance of care? By the way, a place can be too clean. That sounds strange, but it is true. A nursing home is a place where people live. It ought to have a lived-in look about it. If it is too orderly, it may mean there is very little freedom for real living.

SMELL.

One of the real struggles every nursing home deals with is smell. Many patients can no longer control their bladders or their bowels. There will be some smell as a result of this problem. There is smell, and then there is smell. There should not be the strong odor of urine covered up with heavy deodorizers. Good cleaning habits and a well-organized laundry program should leave the home without the presence of strong odors permeating the whole place.

NOISE.

This is a tough one to feel. Happy homes aren't quiet. There is a banter going on between the staff and the residents. There is conversation happening between people, many of whom will be hard of hearing and will talk loudly and must be talked to with some volume. There needs to be some noise, but there also needs to be enough quiet to allow rest. Noise caused by the communication with patients should be a plus. Noise by careless workers banging equipment should be a minus.

BATH FACILITIES

These should be inspected with care. The location, the equipment, and the cleanliness are the most important items. This inspection will probably be a source of reassurance for us. One of the major reasons my mother-in-law became a resident of a nursing home was the availability of bath facilities that fit her needs. Showers and tubs designed so she could be bathed with dignity and care became an important issue when it became evident our facilities were not designed for her comfort or dignity.

MEALS

Let's face it—there is no cooking like home cooking. It is impossible to prepare food in large quantities for a variety of dietary needs and have it taste as good as small portions cooked to order. The question must relate to more than taste. The question must relate to good nutrition, good dietary practice, and the actual eating of the food. Most people who live alone end up not eating very well. It is hard to cook for one person. It is hard to be motivated to cook if one must eat alone. Meals in the nursing home may be a swap-out. We trade some taste for the assurance that the resident is receiving the food he needs to sustain good health.

As we get older, our taste buds deteriorate. Food does not taste the same anymore. Many complaints about food relate to this change more than they relate to the quality of the food.

A large percentage of the residents in a nursing home have false teeth. As we grow older, false teeth become harder to fit and therefore, less efficient. This means the dietitian must plan meals which avoid hard-to-chew foods. This factor along with other factors, such as the need to limit salt and sugar, results in good nutrition with some sacrifice of taste and variety.

It is a good idea to have a meal or so in the home. This will help indicate what kind of quality is there. We will not be left to make judgments based on complaints that may be due to loss of sensitivity to taste or due to a resident using food to express displeasure with being in the home.

After the physical areas have been researched, we should try to get a general feel for the overall attitude of the home. This is a far more subjective judgment. There is no checklist to follow.

One thing to notice is the staff's attitude toward the residents. Recently I walked through a nursing home with an administrator. This remarkable lady called every patient by name and carried on a constant banter with each of them. She teased some. She joked with others. She stopped to chat with another one about a recent illness. I watched the eyes of the residents light up as she talked. I would put a loved one in this home.

I have watched other staff personnel who had the same effect on their residents. This is what I mean about the feel of the place. Visiting families can approach an inspection like a mother-in-law looking for dust and never get the feel of the place. They need to go with an open mind and their feelers out. They need to grasp the feel and then go with the feeling.

Families should look for a home they can join in a mutual task. It will take the work they can do and the work the home can do to meet the needs of the resident. The ideal is for the nursing home and family to combine into a caring partnership.

6. Understanding

May I put the shoe on the other foot? I interviewed several administrators and staff of various nursing homes. I asked them to name their most prevalent problems. As I stated before, the only way to avoid misunderstanding is to have an understanding. It seemed logical that the areas the administrators thought to be their greatest problems would be the areas creating most of the complaints. If these areas create most of the complaint, then they are the areas we are most likely to face.

I was surprised by the response. I expected the greatest problems to be medical concerns, quality of care, or misunderstandings with staff. None of these were mentioned. The problems were more mundane in nature. They were the type of problems any family might face. While the interviews did not bring to light any heady philosophic ideas to discuss, they did bring me face to face with the need to know what to expect before placing a loved one in a nursing home. Maybe a look at the problem areas will give us a realistic look at life in a nursing home. The following problems were included:

LAUNDRY

Laundry topped the list. It seems as if every home has a struggle in this area. This should not be a surprise.

All of us have single socks which will never again be paired with their partners. In spite of ingenious methods devised to keep each person's laundry separate, socks get lost. One large chain finally gave up and began buying socks for all of their residents. They had already tried every other method possible. They had separate little bags for each person's laundry. The laundry was done in the bag. Somehow a sock or a nightgown would escape.

We can take our own precautions. Every item of clothing should be marked. We can do the laundry for our loved one when possible. Beyond this we need to recognize that items get mislaid, even at home.

Beyond the loss of things, we need to recognize that commercial laundry practices are harder on clothes than home laundry practices are. Clothes will not wear as well or as long.

Not understanding this problem in the beginning can lead to a great deal of upset over a lost sock.

RULES

There must be rules if there is to be a sense of order in the large family of a nursing home. Some of these rules are made locally. Many are mandated by state law. An example of rules set by state law would be those governing smoking. Residents are not allowed to smoke in their rooms. The home will provide a smoking area for those who wish to smoke. Cigarettes and lighters must be kept at the nursing station and checked out to the patient one at a time. This can be a source of irritation to those who smoke and are used to smoking when and where they please. Brief thought indicates why the rule is needed. Fire rules demand that smoking be controlled.

We need to spend the time to go over each rule with the staff of the home. We need to be sure that we not only know the rules, but also understand the reasons behind the rules. Too often people ignore the rules upon their entrance to a nursing home and then react when later confronted by the restriction.

THEFT

Things can get stolen. Sometimes there will be residents who are not completely lucid and will take things. Sometimes staff people steal. The staff gets accused far more often than they are guilty.

This is another one of those problems caused by necessary rules. Doors to the resident's rooms cannot be locked in a nursing home. Fire rules alone make locked room doors dangerous. The need to reach the resident for medical reasons also makes unlocked doors a necessity. There will be some losses.

Don't be too quick to decide that everything lost is stolen. Elderly people misplace things and accidents happen. A denture taken from the mouth, wrapped in a napkin, and placed on a food tray can become garbage before it is ever missed.

FOOD

We have already discussed food provided by nursing homes. One problem with food I had not thought of was mentioned by several administrators. Families tend to overdo the snacks for residents. They bring in goodies which the resident devours and then does not eat the meals provided.

I was amazed to hear of how many times a nursing home would have a resident with a serious drinking problem, and family or friends would smuggle in alcohol for the patient.

Snacks are fine, but take care not to make them a substitute for good nutrition.

ROOMMATES

The home we used did not have a private room available, so my mother-in-law had a roommate. They shared a television, even though they had widely varied taste in television programs. They tried conversation even though they had little in common. The roommate had periods when she was difficult to deal with. There was no good solution to this problem. Our position was that if there is no solution to the problem, the only thing to do was to make the best of the situation. We went on with the business of living and managed.

A roommate can cause problems on occasion but also can be a source of positive socialization. One of the major reasons for living in a nursing home is the need for socializing with people of the same age and interest. There are cases of difficult roommates, but there are far more cases of roommates who become fast friends and enjoy each other's company.

CARE

Often there is a wide gap in communication regarding care. Families often want the resident to be super-dependent while the home believes anything a resident can do for himself he should do. Any other approach robs the resident of dignity and purpose.

This gap in philosophy can lead to a great deal of tension. We need to be realistic about what a nursing home is and what it can do. It is not a hospital. It is a home where a loved one lives. The emphasis needs to be on living—living within the limits placed on patients by age and the conditions of health. There needs to be as much independence in this living as possible.

Nursing home administrators place the problem of over protective families high on the list of problems. Often the resident comes to the home after having been cared for with such intensity that they have become increasingly helpless.

There are times when the resident must learn to dress himself. Before patients came to the home, they often could not do this. The family must deal with the resident doing things for the nursing home personnel that the resident would not do for the family. Often the reaction is negative, and the family is critical of the lack of care instead of seeing the positive side of the progress made and the independence gained by the resident.

Sometimes the resident needs to push to gain this independence. This pushing can easily be interpreted as the home not giving proper care.

There will always be legitimate concerns that need to be expressed. When criticism is needed, the family should feel free to express feelings openly to the right people. Take the criticism directly to the administrator. If the administrator is not available, talk to the assistant administrator or the director of nurses. Too often complaints are voiced too far down the line of employees and are never heard by the ones who can make corrections. Criticisms should be voiced—not just hinted. If a change is needed, go immediately to the administrator and share the difficulty in open and direct terms. Instead of making the administrator angry, directness and candor will probably be appreciated.

This chapter has not been a pretty portrayal of life with no problems. If reading this gives a glimpse of reality, then it can be a helpful chapter. We need to enter the nursing home experience with our eyes open and our expectations based on reality.

After listening to the administrators I decided the key word in having a happy experience with a nursing home is flexibility. We must be ready to give and take. The nursing home can't be all we want it to be. The nursing home can't take the place of living at home in good health until we die. The nursing home can be the best option possible when age or health demand a new kind of living.

III. ADJUSTING TO THE DECISION

7. The Adjustment Process

Parents sometimes agree to go to a care facility with almost no argument. Often the decision is theirs from the start. They talk the issues through with logic and clarity. They seem to understand the need to make such a move. After the move is made, some change completely. Often they become hostile and bitter. They accuse their children of forcing them to move into what they now refer to as "this place." The children are left with wonderment and guilt.

Many new residents enter a nursing home with no fuss. After they move in, they still don't raise any overt fuss. They fight the decision in very subtle ways. Hints, criticisms, and martyrdom become the weapons. The children have no way of discerning real problems from masked hostility.

Many parents have claimed all of their lives that they will never live with their children. They always planned to enter a nursing home when the need arose. When the time comes, they feel the pressure to live up to their boast, so they enter a nursing home. Suddenly they begin to accuse their children of not caring or of forcing them to leave their own home where they were happy. The children are left with disbelief and befuddlement.

What happens when people enter a nursing home? Is there a sudden transformation of their characters?

Is there some psychological trauma which sends them into orbit?

Any person placed in a nursing home will go through a period of adjustment. Some people will go through a more intense period than others. Some people will not make the adjustment. What is this adjustment period? What causes it to happen? How long does it last? How do people act during the adjustment period? All these questions need to be answered. Unfortunately, there has been very little study done in this area and very little written to let us understand the process.

People who enter a nursing home go through a period of grief or mourning. I hesitate to use the word grief because it is connected with death in our minds. Grief is the natural response we go through when we suffer loss—any loss. If I lose my billfold, I go through a period of grief. I have a hollow feeling in the pit of my stomach for a day or two, and I feel a sense of loss. If my house burned down, I would feel loss and grief.

Displaced people suffer grief. At a recent conference where I talked about grief to some social workers, we made a startling connection. The social workers served a large number of refugees. They had noticed some patterns in the responses of these people. By comparing what these refugees were feeling with the patterns and responses of grief it became evident that these people were suffering grief. These refugees had lost home, country, culture, relatives, and friends. What else could they feel except grief?

When an elderly person is moved from home, that person loses routine, friends, social position, and turf.

The nursing home resident must go through the grief process in order to adjust to the new order of things. Entering a nursing home is not the real problem. Elderly people would go through the same experience no matter where they moved. The problem is the displacement—not the place.

We must understand this process and allow for it to happen. If we do not understand, we will never handle the experience. Most of the time the children of nursing home residents are unprepared for the responses they meet and end up in a state of panic. The parents may go on through the process and adjust. The children do not see the progress and the adjustment, and they are trapped in a tunnel of guilt with no light at the end.

This is the most important chapter in this book. We must understand the natural process of the grief experience. We must understand the stages our loved ones will go through in this process. We must understand the timetable of grief—how long it will last. We must learn how to recognize the symptoms of a person who is stuck at one stage of grief and making no progress. If we can understand all of this, we can help them move through this process. We can also avoid the panic and guilt as the process goes on.

GRIEF AS A PROCESS

Grief is as natural as eating when you're hungry, snoring when you sleep, or sneezing when your nose itches. It's nature's way of healing a broken heart. There is nothing wrong with grieving. It is healthy. It needs to happen. Too much of the time people try to avoid grief.

Too much of the time society attacks the grieving person. The grief-stricken are told to get hold of themselves. They're told their thinking is not straight. They are told their faith is weak. Too often society's response to grief is, "Buck up and get over it."

If someone is displaced, that person should be sad. That person should cry. That person should complain. Since we do not give people the freedom to grieve, the feeling must come out in some other way.

Most grieving must be done in disguise. There is no way to determine how many complaints about the food, the service, and the treatment in nursing homes is really grief expressing itself in disguise. If people felt free to grieve, there would be less need for the disguise.

The process of grief lasts much longer than most of us suspect. A survey was taken recently that asked people how long the grief of death lasted. The average answer was forty-eight hours. The truth is that grief after death lasts about two years. The grief of displacement probably lasts about the same length of time. No matter how long it lasts, people need to work through the process. We must allow them time.

One thing to remember about people in grief is that they are in transition. They are changing. Where they are today is just where they are today. They will not be there tomorrow. We must not panic. Let them be where they are now and relax. They will not park there. Too often we panic and react. When we do so, they must defend their position. When they defend they park, and the growth process stops.

Grief is a natural process. We must let the process go its own course at its own speed.

THE STAGES OF GRIEF

Some writers on grief have put the process into stages. But the word "stages" conjures up the wrong image. Stages seem to mean there are clear-cut steps people take in grief. The stages are not clear-cut. It is not possible to know when each stage passes. People in grief vacillate between the stages until they gradually move into a new phase. The stages listed here provide a general outline of the whole process. As a general rule, people pass through:

SHOCK.

When a person meets grief or trauma, the mind has a built-in protective system called shock. This is a period of unreality. The person knows what is happening, but it seems like a bad dream that will soon be over.

When a person is confronted with having to be displaced, there is a period of shock. The displaced may agree with very little argument. They may talk about the decision with clear logic. They may even seem anxious to get the move done.

This explains the sudden change some people experience. By the time they move, they may have passed through the shock stage and react with angry feelings which suddenly surfaced.

If there is time between the decision and the move, the shock may wear off before the event. This can cause a person who seemed to be willing to become a most unwilling and stubborn person when the move happens.

If the move is sudden, a person may enter a nursing home with little resistance and then become very hostile a few weeks after the move has occurred.

In almost every case there will be a change when the shock experience wears off.

REALITY.

After the shock experience comes the reality stage. This is the tough one. This is when the totality of the loss hits them. This is when the "poor me" and the "I have been rejected" and the martyrdom begins to be felt and, most of the time, expressed.

This stage is the hardest one of all on the patient. It is also the hardest on the children. If they do not understand that this too shall pass, they can panic and decide they have made a terrible mistake. They can be buried in a sea of guilt and fear.

Thank goodness, this stage will also pass. if we can grit our teeth and steel ourselves, it will pass.

THE REACTION STAGE.

There is anger in grief. There must be anger in grief. The natural response to hurt is anger. Anger in this sense includes words like hurt, frustration, and rejection; these are all the same emotion as anger. People in grief have been hurt, and the hurt produces anger. This anger must focus somewhere, and often they focus on the facility, the staff, the doctors, or on the children who put them into the nursing home.

Handling the anger is so important that we dedicate a full chapter to it in this book. It is imperative that we understand the presence of anger and the necessity for it. If not, we may take it personally and end up hurt by the expressions of the anger.

RECOVERY.

If the process of grief is allowed to reach its natural end, there is a time of recovery. People decide to get well. They decide to live again. This can be a rather sudden and dramatic decision. It can also be a gradual experience. If people are allowed to grieve and to express the grief, they work through the feelings and begin to see things in a different light.

WHAT IF THEY ARE STUCK?

Sometimes people get stuck at one of the stages. They just sit there and will not move. What do family members do then?

We need to understand that not as many are stuck as it may appear. Remember, grief is a long process. Don't be too quick at deciding who is stuck. Give them time. Let it ride for a while and see if they will begin to proceed again.

Often they are not stuck—they are just testing us to see how we will react. They may be seeing what weapons they have to use in manipulating us. *Use Bebe + her mother.*

DO NOT ARGUE WITH THEM.

If we begin to argue, they must begin to defend their position. The defending becomes so important they cannot move without losing a very important battle.

Many people get stuck in the grief process because they have not been allowed to feel and express their true emotions at some point. "Feel what you feel" is a great statement to make to anyone in grief. The statement, "I know you feel that way, and it is certainly understandable," gives the person freedom to forget the defense and move on.

If we have given people time and have not argued and they are still stuck, then what? We can figure out whether or not they are by one simple test. People who are stuck will have a ready argument for why every suggestion will not work. If we suggest that they do something, they will tell us it will not help and why it will not help.

If they are stuck, someone must confront them with the fact that they do not want to get well. When Jesus approached the man at the pool who had been there for thirty-eight years trying to be healed, He asked him what seems to be a rather dumb question. He asked, "Do you want to get well?" That is a great question. Sometimes people must be confronted with the fact that they do not want to be well. The tricky part is deciding who should do the confronting. In most cases it must be the family. It will not be easy. It will not be quick. It will have to happen again and again. The family must begin very lovingly to confront the person with their resistance to getting over it. This is tough love at its toughest.

People will go through a process in adjusting to this new place and way of life. The process is natural; the process is healthy. Older people do not go through this because they are mean. They do not go through this because they are senile. The do not go through this because the facility is bad.

They go through it because they are human beings who have suffered loss. We must accept, understand, and even welcome the process. At the end of the process is recovery.

8. Handling the Anger

Nursing home residents may deny it, hide it, swallow it, or openly express it, but anger is present in displacement. They may not know it, they may not show it, they may disguise it, but anger will be there. Dealing with the anger will be the toughest part of the adjustment to their new home.

When I say anger, I do not mean temper fits. We tend to identify temper and anger as the same emotional expression. Anger in the sense used here means hurt, frustration, rejection, or disappointment.

In a very real sense, the problem with anger will not be expressing too much of it. The problem will be the presence of the anger with no way to express the feelings it causes. Very few people will have the freedom to simply say, "I am mad." A large number will not even realize they are mad. They will be aware of being unhappy or feeling depressed, but they will not connect these feelings to anger.

Those who move to nursing homes who do recognize their anger will probably not know what they are angry about. It is often difficult to identify the anger we feel. If the anger is identified, it is often difficult to find proper ways to express it. If people try to do so, someone will tell them how wrong they are to feel as they do.

In a setting where there can be no expression, the anger must be swallowed. Swallowed anger will either come out in some other way or it will make the person sick. Depression is usually the result of swallowed anger. When we swallow feelings long enough, we begin to go through periods of feeling blue or down. When these periods are ignored, we then experience a shutting off of all feelings. The mind protects itself from going crazy through this process. Depressed people seem to have no emotions left about anything. They seem to lose their ability to care. Emotionally detached probably best describes people suffering from depression caused by swallowed anger.

Anger which is not swallowed will focus somewhere. Often it focuses on an area separate from the real cause of the anger. A nursing home resident may feel angry over the loss of home and friends. If anything is said, the children will feel bad, so nothing is said. The anger then looks for other outlets. It may focus on the nursing home, on a roommate, or the food, or the birds singing outside the window.

It does not have to make sense. Anger is often irrational. Most of the time it will focus on something safe. By safe I mean something that can be complained about without confronting anyone. Many patients find it too painful and risky to tell their children they're mad at them, so they complain to the children about bad food or how the nurses don't care. The anger is expressed, and no one is confronted.

The focus of anger will change. Often people will have several areas of focus. When they talk to the nurses, they complain about the family. When they talk to the family, they complain about the nurses. If one problem is solved, they find another.

When we discover this behavior, it should be evident

that the complaint is a mask hiding the real issue. The issue is anger. What do we do with it?

ANGER MUST BE DISCOVERED AND ALLOWED

The first thing to do in handling another person's anger is to unmask it. People may not know they are angry. They may know it and deny it. They may have been taught all their lives that anger is wrong and bad.

The second thing is to recognize that anger is not wrong. Anger is a natural emotion which needs a natural outlet. Our society has reacted to anger with such horror that it is hard to handle it with any sense of normalcy. People get angry, and they should. When they are angry, they should say so. They should say so without getting a lecture on the evils of anger.

In the case of the nursing home decision, anger is best discovered by someone gently drawing out and helping people involved define their feelings. The gentle drawing out is done through conversation and gradually confronting the real issue. We must be careful not to pick up on their arguments and go chasing after their conversational hooks. They will throw hooks out for us to grab. If we grab one, the conversation is gone. Our side of the conversation will progress something like:

"You seem to be unhappy here. What do you think causes your unhappiness? (No matter what the reasons are, we do not bite.)
"I am sure all of this is so, but how does it make you feel? (Again, no hooks.)
"But how do you feel inside?"

"Do you feel angry?"
"What makes you angry?"
"What about moving here makes you angry?"

It sounds like a broken record repeating the same statement over and over. No matter what is said, we come back to feelings. Don't expect one conversation to accomplish very much. It will be a gradual process over several conversations. The goal is to help them discover what their real feelings are, to express them, and to have them be accepted.

DON'T ARGUE

I said this in the last chapter, but it is so important I must say it again. If we argue with people, they defend. If they defend, a battleground has been formed. Once the battleground is formed, it must be defended until death. If we tell them they are dumb or wrong or senile or mixed up, then they must prove us wrong. If we say, "I can see how you would feel this way— tell me about it," they can proceed to discover the way for themselves with no defense. The more we argue, the more we lose.

THE POWER OF LISTENING

The most powerful part of our bodies is our ears. Nothing changes people quicker or touches them deeper than being listened to. It is easy to prove the power of the ear.

All of us have been angry at some time in our lives. The anger boiled within us for two or three days, and we grew more livid with each passing hour. Finally, we told someone about the anger, and while we were telling it, we could not make it seem as bad as it was. We tried to make it seem horrible, but our hearts were no longer in it. Finally we said something like, "Well, you had to be there," or "It seemed bad at the time." When this happens, we have experienced the power of the ear. As we talked and were heard, the listener's ear drained off the anger. As the anger drained away, our feelings changed.

In dealing with any anger, including that related to the move to a nursing home, the best thing to do is listen. We do not have to have answers. We do not need arguments. We will never win with logic. As they talk and we listen, their anger bleeds off and they discover new concepts. We learn more about ourselves while we are talking than we do while we are being talked to. To let folks talk is to allow them to learn.

They will have anger. If anger is not dealt with, it will focus. When it focuses, whatever it focuses on will catch the wrath of the anger. If someone will listen and they talk it out, the anger can be defined, dealt with, and dissipated.

Dissipated anger is like a spring morning after a thundershower the night before. The storm has passed, and the earth seems to have taken a bath and is squeaky clean.

9. The Guilt Trap

A competent, socially active, intelligent, and perfectly sane woman confessed her problem with guilt to me.

For several years her mother had lived in a nursing home. The home was near her house and since she cared for her mother, she visited every day. These daily visits continued even after the mother lay in a coma. Nothing could be done for the mother. The mother had no idea the visits were taking place, but her daughter went every day.

On Christmas morning she was busy with opening presents, entertaining family, preparing Christmas dinner, and getting ready to entertain out-of-town guests. The time slipped away, and she missed the visit. That day her mother died. The death was a peaceful passage, long-awaited and possibly overdue. Had the lady visited her mother that morning, she would not have noticed any change in her condition. Had she been there when the mother died, there would not have been anything to be done—no help to give, no conscious comfort to administer.

When this woman finally told me her story, she wept as if the event had happened yesterday. Her mother had been dead ten years, but the guilt remained fresh and active.

Anytime a death occurs there will be guilt. If there is none, then we will create it. We just feel the need to feel guilty. We play the game of "if only." "If only" is played when we begin to list all of the things we should have done—"If only I had been there," "If only I had called a doctor," "If only I had been nicer." These are just some of the statements used in the game of "if only." The "if only" is always aimed at us. The game is designed to make us feel a weight of guilt to go along with the weight of grief.

Death is not the only reason we feel guilt. When we make the nursing home decision for a loved one, we will either feel guilt, create guilt, or let someone put a guilt trip on us. Some guilt is normal and natural. The normal and natural will pass as we adjust to the decision. The thing to avoid is the abnormal and unnatural guilt trips we create or we allow others to put on us.

There is a pattern to these guilt traps we get ourselves caught in. In the case of this woman's ten-year struggle with created guilt, four statements sum up the pattern:

1. This was not the first time that the daughter had felt guilty about some part of her relationship with her mother. When someone is trapped as deeply as this daughter was, there is a lifelong pattern of guilt in her past.
2. Guilt is rarely ever logical. The best traps are the most illogical ones.
3. Not all of the trap came from the mother. A great deal of it came from turning her anger inward to focus on herself.
4. Guilt is never constructive. Ten years of guilt created nothing except misery. No one was helped. Nothing was changed. No one was better off.

A great deal of the counseling I do is aimed at helping people handle guilt. Most of this guilt relates to parents. No one can lay guilt on us quite like our parents. No guilt is longer lasting or more devastating than the guilt we grow up with.

If we are faced with the care decision, we are going to be faced with guilt. We must deal with guilt. If it is not dealt with effectively, it can be devastating to us. If it is not conquered, we will find ourselves the victims of a new guilt trip everytime we visit.

People who use guilt to get their way, to get attention, or to create misery seem to become addicted to the use of it. As long as it works, they will continue to use it. When it no longer works, whey will react. The first reaction will be to redouble their efforts at creating guilt. If this does not work, they will try anger. If anger does not work, they will try martyrdom and depression. If none of these work, they're forced to give it up and adjust. The only way the guilt trap can be sprung is for it to quit working. We alone can make it stop. No one can lay guilt on us without our permission. It takes two to create a guilt trip—one who wants to give it and one who is willing to receive it.

Not all parents in a nursing home will use guilt. Most will use it, and most will be successful. Children already feel a sense of frustration, fear, and failure. They already feel as if they have rejected parents by placing them in a nursing home. This makes children ready for guilt trips and guilt traps. It is a rare person who will not use guilt when they have such ready and willing victims.

The guilt will be subtly applied. It is rarely ever presented in a frontal attack. It is applied with hints or unhappiness or pity or stories about how their parents did not have to go to such a place. It can be applied with sugar-sweet kindness—a sort of "I am miserable, but I understand and still love you" kind of stance.

When we react with guilt, we are trapped. It works. It gets attention. It makes us feel miserable. It ensures regular visits, it manipulates us into being angry with the nursing home. It keeps us under control of someone.

Control is the basic idea behind guilt trips. People use guilt to keep control. As long as we feel guilty, we are under their command. Parents have used this tool for years. Why should they stop now? They won't stop as long as it works.

Knowing this will not make the guilt go away. It will help some folks deal with it in a new way, but there will be others who must go deeper into the problem to find a cure. Some folks have a deeper pattern of guilt than others. These people will have the greatest struggle. These are the ones who need to discover:

THE PATTERNS OF GUILT

When we are born, the doctor cuts the cord and sets us free from our mother. He cuts the physical cord. The emotional cord must also be cut. Only the child can cut this cord. There comes a time when we must pull away from our parents emotionally if we are to be whole people—a time when we stop living our lives to please them, a time when we say, "This is me, and you must either accept me as I am or reject me, but I must be me."

This cutting of the cord is a natural process which begins in the teenage years and should be completed by the time we are adults. Sometimes this is an easy and natural process. Sometimes this cutting is encouraged and welcomed by parents. When this is so, we cut away gradually and with their blessing.

Sometimes it is not easy. Sometimes it is civil war. Sometimes it is never done, with disastrous results. It is sad to see grown and married people still desperate for the approval of their parents. It is sad to see them constantly striving for a blessing that will never come. If the blessing is given, then control is lost. Since the issue is control, the blessing will never come.

I have sat with forty-five-year-old men who shared the agony of a father who never told them he loved them.

I have watched the tears of fifty-year-old women who have broken their backs trying to please their mothers, only to be rebuffed again and again.

These are the people who have never found the freedom to be themselves. These are the ones who are on a constant guilt trip. These are the ones who are trapped.

I send these folks back to confront their parents. This is always painful and often is not successful. Whether successful or not, these children have at least begun the process of cutting the cords. This process is long overdue. Since it is overdue, it is a much bigger problem than if it were done sooner. They have years of patterning and anger built-up. The buildup is hard to break through.

The folks who have never cut the cords are the ones who will have the greatest struggle with the guilt of the nursing home decision. They are the ones who have performed all their lives and have struggled all their lives with the cord yet uncut. Now they have made an unpopular decision. This may be the first time they have ever crossed their parents. This may be the first time they have not performed on cue. It is easy to see their dilemma. It is also easy to see their guilt.

In many homes there will be one child who has not cut the cords while the other children have done so long ago. The child who has not cut loose is usually the unblessed child. The unblessed child syndrome occurs in a majority of homes. There is one child who, for some reason, is just not the favorite. This is the odd child. This may be the child who is most like the parents, and they see their own faults in the child. Some unblessed children rebel and leave. Many redouble their efforts to please. They perform for love. When they perform, they become victims of the "no blessing equals control" pattern. As long as they are desperate for the blessing, they are controllable. Since control is the game, the blessing can never be given and the child chases a carrot on a stick for the rest of their lives. The other children go on with their lives and are accepted. This child performs and is not accepted.

Almost invariably, this is the child who will be left with the care of the parents. The other children may put it on this child, or this child may just assume the responsibility. When the care decision comes, it is usually this one who must make it. It is also this one who is most susceptible to guilt.

The struggle with guilt can be deep indeed. It can be very deep for those who have never cut the cord. The cutting is late, they have performed for love, and they are often the unblessed child. The hope is that late or not, these people can confront their parents, declare their independence, and begin the process of breaking free. This will not be easy nor fast nor pleasant, but it will mean they begin to live whole lives. It is time for them to be free.

THE INTERNALIZING OF GUILT

Sometimes guilt does not come from an external source. Sometimes we lay it on ourselves. Often, when people play the game of "if only," they are internalizing their own anger. Anger must focus somewhere. If we do not feel free to be angry externally, we can focus anger on ourselves.

The frustration of the decision, the sense of failure, the feeling of having rejected a parent, and the hurt of the move are all the same emotion as anger. We will have these emotions. If we cannot verbalize them, they may well turn inside. When they turn inside, we begin to fell guilt.

The woman whose mother died on Christmas morning was a victim of internalized guilt. She experienced grief and hurt when her mother died. The grief and hurt quite naturally produced anger. The anger did not seem proper to her, so she could not express it. Her anger focused on herself, and she built up a great case of "if only."

This was not logical, but guilt is rarely logical. The more illogical guilt is, the harder it hits. She spent ten years being miserable with illogical guilt.

We must accept the grief, hurt, and anger as natural results of what we are experiencing. Verbalize it. Shout it out. Tell someone, no matter how silly it sounds or illogical it is. I would rather be silly any day than spend my life with internalized anger creating the "if onlys."

HANDLING GUILT

In addition to the guilt we tend to create for ourselves and internalize, there are three basic sources for the guilt attached to the nursing home decision. The most helpful tool in dealing with these three sources is recognition. We need to identify the guilt sources and recognize that the feelings created by these sources are natural and justified. If we can accomplish recognition, the guilt will be much easier to handle.

The sources are:

GRIEF AND ADJUSTMENT.

This source has already been discussed in detail. It might be helpful at this point to reiterate the importance of our understanding how natural the grief process is. With that understanding, we can avoid panic on our part while the process goes on. If we can recognize the process, accept the necessity of the process, and realize that in most cases the loved one will adjust, then we can relax and avoid guilt.

THE NEW RELATIONSHIP.

As parents get older we tend to find it harder to communicate. At first we think this is caused by their hearing problems or their tendency to get things mixed up. The cause may well be our own discomfort with the changing relationships. Later in this book there is a chapter about the new role and its difficulties. Part of that struggle applies here. We are now called upon to relate as a parent to the person or persons who once were parents to us. We feel hesitant and strange. The discomfort leads us to avoid confrontation. The avoiding leaves us almost speechless. Since we have very little to say we tend to be in a hurry to get away from the discomfort of silence.

People who once had a close relationship that included long talks with their parents can now find conversation stilted and tough. It is easy for us to worry about our discomfort and our need to avoid. If we do not recognize the cause we can fall into a trap of deciding we do not love our parents, a conclusion that can lead us to a great deal of guilt.

The problem of guilt comes from our not realizing that we are not the only people who have experienced this discomfort. Almost everyone goes through a period of adjustment as the roles change; almost everyone goes through a time when conversation is difficult. If we can recognize these truths, we can accept the situation as a normal part of our changing roles and thereby avoid guilt. Then we can move toward learning how to converse in a new relationship. The learning will take time and patience, but it can be done.

UNDERSTANDING THE NORMAL.

We need to avoid the feel-bad-because-we-feel-bad syndrome, which happens when we have a negative thought and then panic. We think we should not think negative thoughts about our loved ones and come to the conclusion that, because we do, there is something wrong with us. In this process we can snowball one thought into major proof of our unworthiness or even insanity. The nursing home decision can create a great deal of feeling-bad-because-we-feel-bad syndromes.

Our discomfort occurs because we do no know what we are supposed to think or feel. We assume that other people do not have the same thoughts or feelings that plague us. We do not feel normal.

I cannot provide a list of all of the feelings we might feel or thoughts we might think, but I can list a couple to give some idea of how normal we really are.

It is normal to be angry. I received a large hug from a woman last week. Her mother, suffering from Alzheimer's disease, was in one wing of a nursing home. Her husband was in another wing suffering with the same disease. She hugged me and said, "Tonight is the first time I have ever heard anyone say it was all right to get mad at them for being sick." She thought no one else in the world would feel anger at sick people.

It is normal to wish things were different. Anytime we are in a pressure situation our minds think of ways to find relief. It is not unusual for families to have thoughts about the relief they would find through the death of a loved one. This does not mean we want that person to die. It does not mean our love has died. It does not mean we are crazy. All these thoughts prove is that we are normal human beings with normal thoughts and feelings.

Guilt is best handled when it is understood. If we can identify the source and recognize that the thoughts and feelings are normal, we can accept ourselves and get on with the business of living. The healthiest stance is one that allows us to tell ourselves that we feel bad because we should do so. If we can handle guilt, we can handle the nursing home decision.

IV. LIVING WITH THE DECISION

10. The Horror Stories

Recently a television station ran a series of programs "exposing" the nursing homes in our area. The promotional ads preceding this series were an example of some of the foolish horror stories surrounding nursing homes. The ads talked of people being left out in the cold. They hinted at widespread mismanagement and "great and grave malpractices." They told of cases in which patients received the wrong medication.

Since I was writing this book, I watched the series with great interest.

My conclusion was that the nursing home should sue the television station for libel. The station ballyhooed much about nothing. No one was left out in the cold. The station showed a woman in a wheelchair sitting outside. Instead of being stranded, she was waiting for her family to drive the car around and pick her up. Station personnel did find a case of wrong medication—one patient received an aspirin by mistake. When the home's manager tried to say this was not the greatest error in the world, the interviewer distorted her explanation.

In light of all the problems with guilt and fear involving the nursing home decision, the series made me angry. It stirred up false fears we could do without. It proved nothing and cured nothing. Most of us don't need any more fears about nursing homes. We have enough already.

We have already heard horror stories about nursing facilities. If these stories are true, then these homes are little more than prisons that torture people. These horror stories add to our fears and make the care decision even harder to make.

This chapter is not a defense of all nursing homes nor an effort to explain away all the problems. Certainly some nursing homes need improvement. Some nursing homes are much better than others. Many things could be improved in almost any nursing home. None claim perfection.

Living with the care decision means we must see these facilities in proper perspective. Part of the problem comes from our own expectations. We expect them to be so much more than they can be. The unmet expectations create anger, the anger creates more anger, and chaos may often result.

We need to understand that these facilities have limitations. They cannot replace a home. "There is no place like home," the song says, and it's true. If we could, we would all stay in our own homes until death do us part. Nothing can take the place of being at home. But we cannot all stay at home. If we live long enough, there will come a time when it's dangerous or physically impossible for us to care for ourselves. When this time comes, we must move to someplace where our needs can be met.

A nursing home can only be the better of the poor options we have. It cannot provide all of the comforts and familiarity of home. It can provide a place for a person to live. It can care for the physical, emotional, social, and spiritual needs and provide friends, activities, and love. But, no matter how well these needs are met, a nursing home can't replace our home. The best thing we can do is realize that nothing can replace home. We could wish the world were different and no one had to ever make these choices, but wishing won't change reality. The choice must be made, and certain things sacrificed in the choosing.

Nursing homes are limited financially. If every home were as plush as we might want and could offer all the services we might wish, very few people could afford to stay there. A realistic approach must be taken to finances. If the homes do not make money, they ultimately cease to exist. If a home is built, it must be financed and the mortgage paid. If the mortgage is to be paid, then the place must be built and staffed within budget limitations. Nursing homes must be constructed so they are available to more than just the wealthy.

Put enough sick people in a place, and it can be somewhat depressing. The turnoff most of us feel when we enter a nursing home is caused by the presence of so many sick people. These people need the care of a nursing facility most. Instead of making us depressed, they should be the source of hope.

I am no longer depressed by nursing homes. One day I saw a nurse lovingly care for an old man I would have had trouble touching. The place became beautiful to me. I now see them as an island of hope. No matter how old or sick I become, there will be a place for me and some people who will care.

Just like any other business, nursing homes are no better than the people they can hire. The staff makes the home. The building can be lovely or tattered—it doesn't really matter. The staff makes the difference.

Just like any other business, the nursing homes have a hard time finding good personnel. Nurses are scarce, caring people are scarce. Finding people who work comfortably with patients is not easy.

We need to realize these limitations and allow for them. Maybe we need to put ourselves in their shoes for a while and decide if we could do better. We do need to check our expectation level. If we can be realistic in the area of expectations, we can probably live with the nursing home decision.

GUILT TRIPS CREATE HORROR STORIES

A woman stood unseen outside the door to her mother's room. She listened in stunned disbelief as her mother worked the nurse over. She had never heard her mother talk this way. She had no idea her mother could be a tyrant. She heard her mother tell the nurse she intended to bump her own leg on the wheel chair and tell her daughter the nurse had hit her.

Lights began to go on in the daughter's mind. She began to understand how deeply she had been duped. While she was present, her mother played the quiet, suffering martyr. When she left, the tyrant came out.

In another instance a woman came to the nursing home each day to change the sheets on her mother's bed. She would then take the sheets home to wash and return them the next morning to repeat the process. She often changed the sheets only minutes after the staff had completed the same task. She told everyone in town how she had to change the sheets or they would not be changed.

One wife told me a horrible tale of a nursing home almost starving her husband to death before she realized what was happening and moved him home.

These horror stories are real, and yet they are not real. To the folks experiencing them, they are real. If the whole story could be told, they are not real. The mother who gave the nurse fits was playing a game with her daughter. The game is called "see how much guilt can be given." She would tell horrid tales which the daughter believed because she could not accept the idea of her mother telling a lie. The daughter would panic and storm into the administration of the home while Mom sat back and enjoyed being in control of all she surveyed.

The lady who changed the sheets was working off her guilt. She needed to do something for her mother to make up for putting her in a nursing home. She also needed to be needed, so the work had to be a necessity. Somehow she convinced herself that the sheets had to be changed. She then tried to convince everyone else.

The man was not being starved, he was starving himself. He knew if he got sick, his wife would take him home and put up with him. Therefore, he would not eat. He got sick. It worked.

There is no way to know how many horror stories we hear about nursing homes come from guilt trips— the guilt traps used by the patients on their families or the ones we inflict on ourselves.

If we make the choice of a nursing facility, then we must take steps to live with the choice. Consider these steps:

CHOOSE WITH CARE.

We need to find the best facility we can. This decision will be governed by our financial condition, availability, the accessibility and convenience, based on our own best judgment.

After the choice is made, we need to relax. We did the best we could, now we either live with the choice or second guess ourselves into a nervous breakdown.

CHECK OUR OWN GUILT.

If we feel guilty, there is no way to please us. We need to work through our guilt. We need to watch ourselves closely, or we may be changing sheets which have just been changed.

KEEP COMMUNICATION LINES OPEN.

If a problem arises, we need to confront it. If we let it slide, it grows. If it grows, we become more angry. If we swallow the anger, it festers until we explode. Explosions rarely hit the real problems, much less cure them. If we have a question, we must ask for an answer. We may feel like a picky pest, but it's better to be a picky pest than an irrational Roman candle blasting off in all directions.

We only have two options: to confront or to manipulate. We manipulate by hinting instead of saying— by swelling up instead of expressing. Manipulation never works, so we end up even more frustrated. If we have a question, we must speak up.

PARTICIPATE AND BE INVOLVED.

I have spoken to the residents at a nursing home one night each month for nine years. This participation changed my life. I became involved in the lives of some very remarkable people. They gave me hope. Once I feared old age, but they showed me there is nothing to fear. I know the joys and sorrows, the ups and downs, the good and the bad of this group of folks. I would not trade this experience.

The best thing we can do is participate in the nursing home. If our only participation is with the relatives we have there, we see only a small part of the whole picture. By getting involved, we begin to see the whole story. We can begin to see beyond the setting, the schedules, and food to the people. The results can be amazing.

We may sit back and knock the place and never run out of complaints. But, if we participate, we may change some things for the better and at least understand the situation.

Using a nursing facility allows us the freedom to spend more quality time with our loved ones. While the nursing home staff takes care of their physical needs, we can concentrate our efforts in other areas. This leaves us free to do enjoyable things we might not have the time or energy to do if we provided the physical care. This gives us a chance to be a welcome visitor and creator of good times.

If we can get the guilt and adjustments out of the way, our visits can be happy times. Children sometimes place parents in nursing homes and forget them. I think this happens because each visit creates guilt in the children, and therefore they avoid the unpleasant task of visiting.

If this hurdle can be crossed, we may have a great deal of fun being involved in the life of a loved one. We can plan times for a visit to our homes. These visits don't have to be extended visits, but they can be great experiences.

One woman I know periodically loads up a carload of people from a nursing home and takes them out for hamburgers. She discovered these folks crave an occasional hamburger. She also found out that she looks forward to this fun time for herself.

I read the other day about a grade school producing a musical program using students and the residents of a nursing home. The music may not have been the greatest, but the fun was tops.

We could do many fun things with our loved one and with other nursing home residents. They need our involvement and so do we.

Someone has said they would rather light one candle than curse the darkness. This is a good place to start lighting candles.

11. The Changes

I wish everyone could have known my mother-in-law. She was one of the most delightful women God ever put together. Her laugh could be heard a block away. She cared for people and showed her caring. I wish I had all the money she spent on food for people who were in need. She furnished a ham for the family dinner at many, many funerals in her hometown.

She kept up with so many people we finally had to resort to mimeographing newsletters during her illness. Every birthday brought more than forty cards. I loved her, and so did everyone who knew her well.

In the hospital and later in the nursing home, she became a selfish, complaining, demanding, and whining old woman. Nothing seemed good enough. She complained of slow nurses. She expected her daughters to be present at all times. If her daughters could not be present, then nurses must be hired. The nurses were met with complaints and demands.

A few years earlier she would have been a model patient. Everyone in the hospital would have known her and would have loved her. She would have been interested in the welfare of other patients in the hospital and would have been so involved with their needs she would not have had time to worry about herself.

I knew changes occurred in people as they aged. I knew these changes were often hard to accept. When

I faced them, I found them much harder to accept than anticipated.

I had dealt with some of the changes brought on by aging through my parents. These changes were gradual and accepted as normal. I knew communication became more difficult as people grew older. I had experienced the gradual hardening of attitudes and opinions through the aging process of my parents and others.

I could accept these changes because they were gradual and natural. However, the changes in my mother-in-law came suddenly and unexpectedly. These dramatic changes boggled my mind.

My wife and I struggled before we could adjust to these changes. At first we tried to explain them away. We searched for explanations. It seemed to us that if we could find a logical explanation it would somehow make the changes clear up. Every possible explanation was explored, discussed, dissected, and finally discarded.

We tried to tell ourselves that these changes were temporary. We hoped each day would bring a return of the delightful personality we had known, but as time passed the old personality didn't return. We found ourselves pushed in a corner. We could no longer deny the changes. We could not continue to hope for a sudden reversal. We found it difficult to blame all the changes on medication. The medication changed, but the strange behavior remained the same.

Like it or not, we had to adjust. We gradually were able to come to grips with the changes and accept them. We then had to figure out how to handle this new, demanding person and how to respond to her demands. Even after we adjusted, we still wondered what caused these dramatic changes.

There are a lot of causes for these changes and one cause is the real culprit. Stated simply, people change because they begin to live on a survival level.

A lot of people who seem to be selfish are not really selfish. They are surviving. Survival is one of the basic drives within the human being. When threatened, our instinct to survive takes over. While striving to survive we will be selfish. If we are trapped in a burning building, our first reaction is to save ourselves.

Some people never rise above the survival level of living. Insecurities and fears dominate their whole lives. These fears become so important they can not think of anything else. Their need to survive overshadows the feeling and need of others.

Others rise to live on a higher level. They conquer enough of their fears and grow out of enough of their insecurities so they can turn outward to others. They notice others because they are not dominated by self-interest needs. They have learned how to get themselves off of their hands. My mother-in-law was one who lived on a higher level until late in her life.

Even those who rise to a higher level can be pushed into survival if they meet enough fear and insecurity. Someone's death can put them into the survival mode, at least for a time. Illness can scare them deeply enough to bring out the instinct to save themselves. A move from home can also cause this. These people are not mean, they are scared. They are insecure.

This happened to my mother-in-law. All her life she had been self-reliant and secure. She lived free to do as she pleased in her own way. Suddenly she lost her health. She couldn't take care of herself. She had to face the fact that she would not get well. She faced major surgery with little hope for improvement. The insecurity, the pain, and the fear drove her to survive. Surviving is always selfish.

Our tendency is to argue with these people. We tell them how selfish they are. We shame them. We disagree with their logic. The more we argue, the more they must defend. When they defend, they are locked into surviving deeper than ever.

These people need understanding and acceptance more than argument. They need someone to draw out their fears—someone who will ignore their demanding and ask them how they really feel. They don't understand what's going on inside of themselves, and they need to explore it for themselves. If they can begin to deal with their true feelings and understand where they are, they can begin the climb back to another level.

If we allow the changes to affect us, they can become a system of control. If the control works, they will naturally use it. If we can be kind but firm, they cannot use demands to control us. If the control does not happen, then they must change.

My wife handled the changes beautifully. She cared and gave of herself, but she did not allow any guilt trips. She did what she could and gave what she felt she could give. She would not go beyond this and refused to feel guilty about not doing more. Through it all she was kind, but firm. She understood the concept of love being tough. When she would not perform to the total demands, her mother sent for her other daughter. My wife did not take this as a putdown or allow guilt to develop. She continued to do what she could and no more. She kept on loving without buying into the pressure or the guilt. When her mother died, my wife refused to play the "if only" game. She had done what she could, and that was enough. Her conscience remained clear.

The changes came and were accepted, we adjusted, and lived with them. A lot of folks I know need to experience this same process.

12. The New Role

I picked up a book not too long ago that was a pictorial history of the last days of an old man. The two grandsons of the man were free-lance photographers who decided to record the passage of their grandfather. They decided to keep the man in their home and care for him. The pictures are warm at times and tough at other times. They did not gloss over the rough areas of caring for a dying man. They recorded the loss of mental competence, the need for the old man to be watched constantly, and even the habit the old man acquired of taking off all his clothes.

The message of the book seemed to be that this was the answer to caring for aging people in our families. There was another message revealed in the book. This message was the wear and tear on the grandmother and the families of the grandsons. The book records the gradual fraying of nerves and the loss of respect.

The book reminded me of the last years of my grandfather. A delightful and tough little man, he lived to be ninety-eight. In his last years he became a demanding, almost impossible patient. He was almost totally deaf and very hard to handle.

Two of my aunts left their homes to care for their father. This care lasted over three years. They made this move because they could not stand the thought of putting their father in a nursing home. They put him in a nursing home for a brief time, but he complained so they moved him to his home and moved in with him for the duration of his life. The two aunts have been considered family heroines because of their concern and care. I wonder if the sacrifice was wise.

The wear and tear on these two women could never be estimated. The cost to their families may have been even higher. They did not know it at the time, but they did not have very many years left to live with their husbands. Both men died within a few years of my grandfather's death. If the cost could have been confined to the lives of the two aunts, then it might be different. But it could not. Their husbands were cheated out of three years when they did not have many years to spend. Their lives were also important, and their needs also mattered. Their lives and needs were ignored in the intense drive to take care of Grandpa.

One thing is evident in the book and in the experience with my grandfather—the roles become reversed. In the book there are two pictures that say a thousand words. One picture shows the grandfather holding a grandson who was about three years of age. The other picture shows the grandson carrying the grandfather to bed. Those pictures convey the meaning, "We are cared for, and then we return the caring." The other message is, "There comes a time when the parents are no longer in the role of parent, and the children must assume the guardian role."

When children assume the role, they feel inadequate and strange. Making decisions frightens them. They think they should perform in some set manner, but the methods of this performance remain undefined. They feel lost and confused. They wish someone would tell them what to do. They long for parents to once again be parents and tell them what to do.

We must make decisions based on the best options available. The decisions should be logical. The nursing home decision must consider the cost to everyone involved. We do not have the right to demand that others pay a cost which is unfair to them. At this point, love gets tough. This is when love must do what people need—not necessarily what they want. The decision must be made to allow everyone concerned to have a life. It may not be an ideal life or the one we would all want, but at least the best life available. We all need to live.

And after the decision is made—relax.

13. Purpose

She did not seem to be particularly old. I was shocked to find she had retired. She was as sharp as she was witty, and even though she was the only mature person in a retreat for young people, she kept us on our toes. She joined in the small group discussion, and her two cents' worth was always worth at least a quarter. She seemed to have it all together. Somehow the discussion turned serious, and she suddenly seemed frail and vulnerable. We began to realize how much she hurt and how well she hid the pain.

She told us about aging. Not the normal stuff about lost memory, lost teeth, and various aches and pains. She cut through to the heart of the matter. She said, "The roughest part of aging is living without goals. All my life I was looking forward to something. First it was getting out of college, then marriage, then a new home, then a family, then the marriage of my children, then the empty nest and time to travel with Bob. Bob is gone, I am retired, and all I can do is look back. There is nothing to look toward except the day I am to die. I have lost my purpose. The rest of it I can handle. So what if the old body creaks a little. The loss of purpose leaves me with no reason to live and no way to die."

Purpose is the number one need of us all. The need is particularly acute in the elderly, but it is not limited to any age group. I know a number of young men who struggle deeply in their search for purpose. "Why am I here?" is a question asked in boardrooms as well as nursing homes. We are victims of the puritan work ethic. Somehow our sense of value got tied to what we do instead of what we are. We are valuable if we are doing something. We are not valuable if we are doing nothing. Our value is based on performance. When two people meet for the first time, the first question most often asked is, "What do you do?" If the answer is some important task, the person is viewed as important. If the task makes a lot of money, the person is viewed as some kind of superperson. If the task is menial, then the person is viewed as menial. The important person might be a scoundrel and the menial person might be a saint, but these qualities have very little effect on the value placed on them. We are what we do.

This ethic works fairly well for part of our lives. It drives us to strive for excellence. It pushes us to climb the social ladders in an effort to find worth. The ethic begins to wear thin in middle age, and we begin to question the meaning of life. We can usually weather the storm and push on. The ethic fails when we can no longer perform. Suddenly we are no longer among the doers of the world, and we are left with nothing to base our value upon. The result is we are left with no purpose. Life begins to be a look backward.

Somehow we need to discover that our worth is in who we are. We are here on this earth to become. Everything that happens to us is part of this becoming. We are becoming as long as we are breathing. Becoming does not stop when we retire. Becoming does not stop when illness starts. Becoming is a lifelong process, and the becoming is the purpose for our being.

I do not believe in reincarnation. Once is enough as far as I am concerned. There is one concept of reincarnation I like. What if this is the fifth time through for me. Each trip is designed to see how far I can progress, how kind I can become, or what kind of caring person I can develop into. This concept puts purpose in the right perspective. I am not here to be successful at a job. I am here to develop a person into the best and highest person possible.

When my father-in-law retired, I was in fear for his life. I did not think he would live five years past retirement. He had been a very successful director of a company. The job had become his life, and his value rested in the position he held and the performance he gave.

A few years after retirement he became ill. The illness ultimately took his life. When my granddaughter was three months old, I took her to his house for a visit. As we talked he began to tell me how helpless and useless he felt. He listed all the things he could no longer accomplish. I made a speech to him that I wish could be heard and grasped by the whole world.

I said, "I brought my granddaughter to see you today. I did so because she needs to meet you. She needs to know you now and will need to know you for the rest of her life. As she grows I will tell her about you. I will not tell her what you did for a living. I will tell her how you lived. I will tell her who you were. I will tell her about you kindness, your love, your dedication to truth. These things are who you are and what makes you of value."

We embraced, and I hoped he could find some purpose in who he was.

I made a list of the ten most influential people in

my life. No one on the list was successful in terms of jobs held or money earned. They were people who had warmth, concern, and knew how to love. This leads me to believe that if someone is kind, that person is among the most valuable people in the world. I marvel at how some folks can live in a hard world and remain soft, in a cruel world and remain kind, in a selfish world and somehow still be able to love.

Somehow we need to help our elderly loved ones grasp these concepts. They need to feel a sense of worth and purpose. If they cannot discover a basis for worth and purpose, their lives can easily become a sordid wait for the end. In most cases this must be a rediscovery. Usually they will have lived their lives in a "beauty is as beauty does" sort of world. We can help them discover a "beauty is as beauty is" sort of world.

There is one key word in this effort. The word is affirmation. Nothing works as well as the proper use of this great word. Jesus was the master user of affirming. He had a knack for pointing out the strengths of people, even weak people. He began to call a follower Peter, which meant "rock" a long time before Peter was very rocky. That is affirmation.

Some time spent with an elderly loved one pointing out what value they have been to us can do wonders. I told one that because of their example I no longer feared old age. We can tell them how proud we are to be a part of their lives. We can tell them they are needed.

They are needed. They are still becoming, and we can learn much by being a part of the process. If we are alive, we aren't through.

Epilogue

Every author has a dream for his work. I am no exception. I, too, have a dream.

I dream of this book helping people with a most difficult decision, a decision that almost automatically places a load of guilt on the ones who must decide. I dream of great loads of guilt being laid aside.

I dream of this book being read by folks who are faced with going to live in a nursing home. I dream of these folks beginning to understand their own feelings and the feelings of others.

I dream of nursing home personnel reading these pages and understanding a little more about their residents and the families they serve.

Above all, I dream of families and nursing homes becoming care teams—together providing love and care for the remarkable and resilient folks who live in a new place and yet still live.

If any of these dreams are fulfilled, I will be filled to the full.

Doug Manning